# This Ramadan
# Activity Book belongs to:

Maira and Aamir

# Some Hadith About Ramadan:

When the month of Ramadan starts, the gates of Heaven are opened and the gates of Hell are closed and the devils are chained. (Bukhari and Muslim)

Abu Huraiyra ؓ related that the Prophet ﷺ said, "Whoever fasts during Ramadan with faith and seeking his reward from Allah will have his past sins forgiven. Whoever prays during the nights in Ramadan with faith and seeking his reward from Allah will have his past sins forgiven. And he who passes Laylat ul Qadr in prayer with faith and seeking his reward from Allah will have his past sins forgiven." (Bukhari and Muslim)

Anas ؓ related that the Prophet ﷺ said, "Take the Suhoor meal, for there is blessing in it." (Bukhari and Muslim)

Salman ibn Amir Dhabi ؓ related that the Prophet ﷺ said, "Break your fast with dates, or else with water, for it is pure." (Abu Dawud and Tirmidhi)

Zaid ibn Khalid Juhni ؓ related that the Prophet ﷺ said, "He who provides for the breaking of the fast of another person earns the same merit as the one who was fasting, without diminishing in any way the reward of the latter." (Tirmidhi). *This means that the person who feeds a fasting person at Iftaar will receive the same reward as the person who was fasting, and the fasting person's reward will not be any less.*

"Whoever fasts Ramadan with imaan and the hope of reward will be forgiven his previous sins." (Ibn Majah)

# Essential Ramadan Du'as:

Before Fasting:

$$\text{اَللّٰهُمَّ اَصُوْمُ غَدًا لَكَ فَاغْفِرْلِيْ مَا قَدَّمْتُ وَمَا اَخَّرْتُ}$$

*O Allah! I shall fast tomorrow for Your sake, so forgive my future and past sins.*

Alternatively, recite this du'a:

$$\text{بِصَوْمِ غَدٍ نَّوَيْتُ}$$

*I intend to fast tomorrow.*

On Breaking your Fast:

$$\text{اَللّٰهُمَّ لَكَ صُمْتُ وَبِكَ اٰمَنْتُ وَعَلٰى}$$
$$\text{رِزْقِكَ اَفْطَرْتُ}$$

*O Allah! I fasted for You. In You do I believe, and with your provision (food) do I break my fast.*

After Iftaar:

$$\text{ذَهَبَ الظَّمَأُ وَابْتَلَّتِ الْعُرُوْقُ وَثَبَتَ الْاَجْرُ}$$
$$\text{اِنْ شَاءَ اللّٰهُ}$$

*The thirst has gone, the throat is not dry and the reward has been earned, if Allah so wills.*

**Before Eating:**

بِسْمِ اللهِ وَعَلٰي بَرَكَةِ اللهِ

*In the name of Allah and upon the blessings of Allah.*
*Whoever reads this du'a will receive blessings in their meals.* (Al-Hisnul Haseen)

**After Eating:**

اَلْحَمْدُ لِلهِ الَّذِيْ اَطْعَمَنَا وَسَقَانَا وَجَعَلَنَا مِنَ الْمُسْلِمِيْن

*All praise be to Allah who gave us food and drink and made us Muslims.*
*Allah becomes pleased when His slave praises Him after meals.* (Al-Hisnul Haseen)

**When Eating as a Guest at Someone Else's Home:**

اَللّٰهُمَّ بَارِكْ لَهُمْ فِيْمَا رَزَقْتَهُمْ وَاغْفِرْ لَهُمْ وَارْحَمْهُمْ

*O Allah, bless them in what You have provided them with, amd forgive them, and have mercy upon them.*

اَكَلَ طَعَامَكُمُ الْاَبْرَارُ وَصَلَّتْ عَلَيْكُمُ
الْمَلَائِكَةُ وَاَفْطَرَ عِنْدَكُمُ الصَّائِمُوْنَ

*May the righteous partake of your food and the angels of mercy descend upon you and those fasting break their fast with you.*

**Before Wudhu:**

بِسْمِ اللهِ وَالْحَمْدُ لِلهِ

*(I commence wudhu) in the name of Allah the Great, and all praise be to Allah (for keeping me faithful) in the Deen (religion) of Islam.*

**After Wudhu:**

اَشْهَدُ اَنْ لاَّ اِلهَ اِلاَّ اللهُ وَحْدَهُ لاَ شَرِيْكَ لَهُ

وَاَشْهَدُ اَنَّ مُحَمَّدًا عَبْدُهُ وَرَسُوْلُهُ

اَللّٰهُمَّ اجْعَلْنِي مِنَ التَّوَّابِيْنَ وَاجْعَلْنِيْ مِنَ

الْمُتَطَهِّرِيْنَ

*O Allah, make me of the repenters and make me of the purified.*
*The eight doors of Jannah will be opened for the one who recites this du'a and he will have the choice to enter from whichever door he wishes. (Tirmidhi)*

**On Awakening:**

اَلْحَمْدُ لِلهِ الَّذِىْ اَحْيَانَا بَعْدَ مَا اَمَاتَنَا وَاِلَيْهِ النُّشُوْرُ

*All praise is due to Allah who has given us life after death and to Him is the return after death.*

**Before Sleeping:**

اَللّٰهُمَّ بِاسْمِكَ اَمُوْتُ وَاَحْیٰی

*Oh Allah, with Your name do I die and live.*

**When Entering the Masjid:**

اَللّٰهُمَّ افْتَحْ لِيْ اَبْوَابَ رَحْمَتِكَ

*O Allah, open for me the doors of Your mercy.*

**When Leaving the Masjid:**

اَللّٰهُمَّ اِنِّي اَسْئَلُكَ مِنْ فَضْلِكَ

*O Allah, verily I seek from You, Your bounty.*

**For an Increase in Knowledge:**

رَبِّ زِدْنِيْ عِلْمًا

*Oh My Lord, increase me in knowledge.*

**At Sunset:**

اَللّٰهُمَّ هٰذَا اِقْبَالُ لَيْلِكَ وَاِدْبَارُ نَهَارِكَ
وَاَصْوَاتُ دُعَاتِكَ فَاغْفِرْلِيْ

*O Allah, this is approaching of Your night and the disappearing of Your day and the sounds of those who pray to You. So do forgive me.*

# Day 1

Alhumdulillah for: _making first fast easy_

Today's du'a: Ya'Allah, Let COVID-19 go extinct, and let our fasts be easier. Ameen.

## The Fastometer
Color in the amount that you fasted today

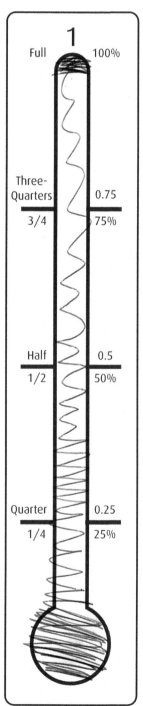

## Sadaqah Stars
Write down three good deeds that you did today

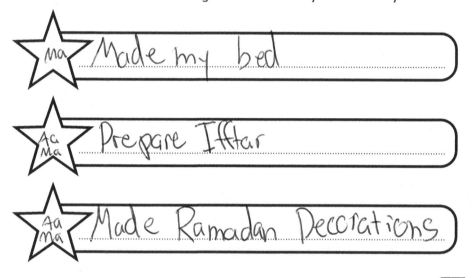

Made my bed

Prepare Iftar

Made Ramadan Decorations

Number of Qur'an pages that you read: ⟨1⟩

## Color in the salah that you prayed
_(it doesn't matter if you prayed at home, school or at the masjid)_

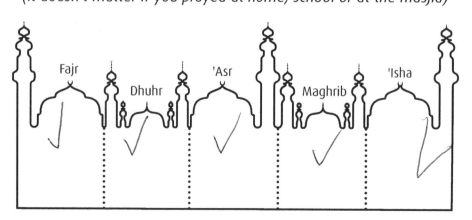

Fajr ✓   Dhuhr ✓   'Asr ✓   Maghrib ✓   'Isha ✓

# Design Time

Design a new masjid:

**Masjid name:** Masjhid Allah (SWT)

# Day 2

Alhumdulillah for: ...........................................................................

Today's du'a: *May everybody stay safe. Ameen.*

## The Fastometer
Color in the amount that you fasted today

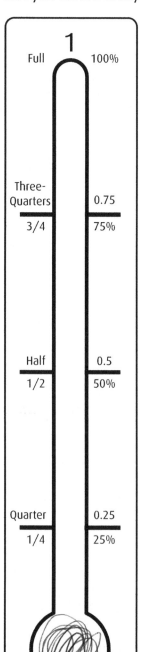

Full — 1 — 100%

Three-Quarters — 0.75
3/4 — 75%

Half — 0.5
1/2 — 50%

Quarter — 0.25
1/4 — 25%

## Sadaqah Stars
Write down three good deeds that you did today

Number of Qur'an pages that you read: ⟨3⟩

## Color in the salah that you prayed
*(it doesn't matter if you prayed at home, school or at the masjid)*

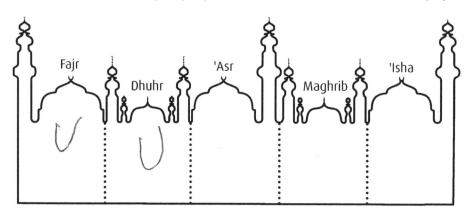

Fajr    Dhuhr    'Asr    Maghrib    'Isha

# True or False

| | True | False |
|---|---|---|
| 1. Ramadan falls in the month of May every year. | | |
| 2. You have to fast from sunset to sunrise. | | |
| 3. When you wake up to start your fast, this is called Iftaar. | | |
| 4. It is sunnah to break your fast with dates. | | |
| 5. If you do anything good in Ramadan, your reward is multiplied by 70. | | |
| 6. Fasting is one of the five pillars of Islam. | | |
| 7. Ramadan is also known as the "Month of the Qur'an". | | |
| 8. In Arabic, the word 'fasting' is known as "Sawm". | | |
| 9. Ramadan is the first month of the Islamic calendar. | | |
| 10. Fasting is an act of worship. | | |

# Day 3

Alhumdulillah for: ........................................................................................

Today's du'a: ........................................................................................

........................................................................................

........................................................................................

## The Fastometer
Color in the amount that you fasted today

1

Full          100%

Three-Quarters     0.75
3/4            75%

Half           0.5
1/2            50%

Quarter        0.25
1/4            25%

## Sadaqah Stars
Write down three good deeds that you did today

☆ ........................................................................................

☆ ........................................................................................

☆ ........................................................................................

Number of Qur'an pages that you read: ⬡

## Color in the salah that you prayed
*(it doesn't matter if you prayed at home, school or at the masjid)*

Fajr     Dhuhr     'Asr     Maghrib     'Isha

# Math Task

Qur'ans are all split into 30 chapters, also known as 'para' or 'juz'.
If each juz is 28 pages, let's do some sums.

1. How long would it take to pray a juz, if you prayed 7 pages per day?

2. How long would it take to pray a juz, if you prayed 14 pages per day?

3. How long would it take to pray a juz, if you prayed 4 pages per day?

4. How many weeks would it take to pray the full Qur'an if you prayed 4 pages per day?

5. If you prayed 5 juz per month, how many times could you complete the Qur'an in a year?

# Day 4

Alhumdulillah for: ...........................................................................................

Today's du'a: ...........................................................................
...........................................................................................
...........................................................................................

## The Fastometer
Color in the amount that you fasted today

## Sadaqah Stars
Write down three good deeds that you did today

☆ ...........................................................................................

☆ ...........................................................................................

☆ ...........................................................................................

Number of Qur'an pages that you read: ⬡

## Color in the salah that you prayed
*(it doesn't matter if you prayed at home, school or at the masjid)*

Fajr    Dhuhr    'Asr    Maghrib    'Isha

**1**
Full — 100%

Three-Quarters — 0.75
3/4 — 75%

Half — 0.5
1/2 — 50%

Quarter — 0.25
1/4 — 25%

# Design Time

Design a poster encouraging people to attend the masjid you designed:

# Day 5

Alhumdulillah for: .......................................................................................

Today's du'a: ...........................................................
...............................................................................
...............................................................................

## The Fastometer
Color in the amount that you fasted today

## Sadaqah Stars
Write down three good deeds that you did today

☆ .......................................................................

☆ .......................................................................

☆ .......................................................................

Number of Qur'an pages that you read: ⬡

## Color in the salah that you prayed
*(it doesn't matter if you prayed at home, school or at the masjid)*

Fajr      Dhuhr      'Asr      Maghrib      'Isha

**1**

Full — 100%

Three-Quarters — 0.75
3/4 — 75%

Half — 0.5
1/2 — 50%

Quarter — 0.25
1/4 — 25%

# Good Deed Task

Bake some chocolate cupcakes and share with your neighbors.

## Ingredients:

- 4oz butter, softened. You can microwave for 10 seconds.
- 4oz sugar. Try to use unrefined sugar if you can!
- 2 eggs
- 3oz self-raising flour
- 1oz cocoa
- 2 tablespoons boiling water. You will need an adult helper to do this for you.
- Cupcake tray, for 12 cupcakes
- 12 cupcake cases

## Method:

1. Pre-heat your oven to Gas Mark 6 / 200°C / 400°F.

2. In a large bowl, whisk together the butter and sugar until light and fluffy.

3. Add in the eggs and whisk. If there is any butter stuck to the sides of the bowl, scrape it off with a spatula then whisk again until the mixture is smooth.

4. Slowly add in the flour and cocoa, and ask an adult to put the boiling water in. Mix well.

5. Line a cupcake tray with the cases, then spoon in your mixture - approximately 1 tablespoon per case.

6. Put in the oven and bake for approximately 15 minutes. You can ask your adult helper to put a toothpick into one of the cakes and if it comes out clean then they are done.

7. Decorate! You can decorate with melted chocolate and sprinkles, jam and whipped cream (only when the cakes are cool, or the cream will melt), or put a marshmallow on top of each cake as soon as they are out of the oven.

8. Share - this is the most important part!

# Day 6

Alhumdulillah for: .................................................................

Today's du'a: .............................................................
.............................................................
.............................................................

## The Fastometer
Color in the amount
that you fasted today

## Sadaqah Stars
Write down three good deeds that you did today

☆ .............................................................

☆ .............................................................

☆ .............................................................

# Number of Qur'an pages that you read: ⬡

# Color in the salah that you prayed
*(it doesn't matter if you prayed at home, school or at the masjid)*

Fajr    Dhuhr    'Asr    Maghrib    'Isha

**The Fastometer**

| | 1 | |
| Full | | 100% |
| Three-Quarters | | 0.75 |
| | 3/4 | 75% |
| Half | | 0.5 |
| | 1/2 | 50% |
| Quarter | | 0.25 |
| | 1/4 | 25% |

# Coloring Page

# Day 7

Alhumdulillah for: ........................................................

Today's du'a: ........................................................
........................................................
........................................................

## The Fastometer
Color in the amount that you fasted today

## Sadaqah Stars
Write down three good deeds that you did today

☆ ........................................................

☆ ........................................................

☆ ........................................................

Number of Qur'an pages that you read: ⬡

## Color in the salah that you prayed
*(it doesn't matter if you prayed at home, school or at the masjid)*

Fajr    Dhuhr    'Asr    Maghrib    'Isha

**Fastometer:**
1    100%    Full
Three-Quarters    0.75    3/4    75%
Half    0.5    1/2    50%
Quarter    0.25    1/4    25%

# Wordsearch

All About Ramadan

| S | Z | G | H | K | L | F | T | U | H | A | J | J | U | D | G | H |
|---|---|---|---|---|---|---|---|---|---|---|---|---|---|---|---|---|
| Q | A | Y | U | I | O | A | A | V | M | Z | X | D | T | H | J | J |
| A | K | D | A | T | E | S | S | U | H | A | O | P | Q | S | M | L |
| C | A | F | H | A | T | T | G | S | Z | Q | S | E | U | K | J | K |
| N | T | P | R | Q | U | I | S | U | X | C | V | J | R | I | M | B |
| Q | T | U | N | W | H | N | V | H | W | X | Q | Y | I | N | Z | A |
| U | B | C | F | A | A | G | D | O | E | G | I | H | N | D | J | M |
| R | E | V | E | L | A | T | I | O | N | P | R | H | O | N | L | N |
| A | I | O | R | P | J | Z | Q | R | X | G | T | O | O | E | X | S |
| N | F | U | R | A | Y | X | U | Z | A | F | A | B | J | S | M | A |
| N | T | Q | D | I | T | O | P | O | F | H | R | Z | Q | S | S | L |
| O | A | E | F | D | S | G | I | F | T | S | A | B | A | I | A | A |
| R | A | M | A | D | A | N | H | G | F | E | W | C | D | O | L | R |
| P | R | S | U | P | P | L | I | C | A | T | I | O | N | N | A | O |
| R | S | U | D | O | O | W | F | C | V | B | H | N | M | A | H | O |
| S | F | C | H | A | R | I | T | Y | Y | N | M | U | I | O | H | R |
| Q | O | R | A | B | D | N | J | K | T | Y | S | G | H | W | N | B |

| Charity | Kindness | Suhoor |
| Dates | Masjid | Salah |
| Fasting | Quran | Tuhajjud |
| Gifts | Ramadan | Tarawih |
| Iftaar | Revelation | Zakat |

# Day 8

Alhumdulillah for: .................................................................................

Today's du'a: ......................................................
..............................................................................
..............................................................................

## Sadaqah Stars
Write down three good deeds that you did today

☆ ..............................................................................

☆ ..............................................................................

☆ ..............................................................................

## Number of Qur'an pages that you read: ⬡

## Color in the salah that you prayed
*(it doesn't matter if you prayed at home, school or at the masjid)*

Fajr    Dhuhr    'Asr    Maghrib    'Isha

## The Fastometer
Color in the amount
that you fasted today

1

| Full | 100% |
| Three-Quarters | 0.75 |
| 3/4 | 75% |
| Half | 0.5 |
| 1/2 | 50% |
| Quarter | 0.25 |
| 1/4 | 25% |

# Missing Words

Fill in the blanks to work out the correct words and learn all about Ramadan.

Ramadan is the n____ month of the Islamic c_____, when Muslims all around
the w____ fast between s_____ and s_____.

Ramadan is one of the five p_____ of Islam.

The Q____ was first revealed to the Prophet M_____ during the month of
Ramadan. Laylat ul Qadr ('The Night of P____') is the actual night that the Qur'an
was revealed.

Almost all Muslims try to give up b__ habits during Ramadan, and some will try to
become b_____ Muslims by p_____ more or reading the Qur'an. Many Muslims
will attempt to read the wh___ of the Qur'an at least once during this s_____
month.

The meal just before sunrise is known as S_____ and the meal directly after sunset
is known as I_____.

Fasting reminds Muslims of the p___ people around the world who don't have
anything to e__ all year round. This teaches us to appreciate and not w____ what
we have and to be k___ to others. Muslims fast to please Allah.

# Day 9

Alhumdulillah for: .................................................................................

Today's du'a: .................................................................................
.................................................................................
.................................................................................

## The Fastometer
Color in the amount that you fasted today

## Sadaqah Stars
Write down three good deeds that you did today

Number of Qur'an pages that you read:

## Color in the salah that you prayed
*(it doesn't matter if you prayed at home, school or at the masjid)*

Fajr    Dhuhr    'Asr    Maghrib    'Isha

1
Full          100%

Three-Quarters          0.75
3/4          75%

Half          0.5
1/2          50%

Quarter          0.25
1/4          25%

# Math Task

Work out the Sadaqah jar mathematics.

$10 + 15 + 65 +$ ___ $=$ **100**

$7 \times 4 =$

$17 + 23 + 15 +$ ___ $=$ **80**

$9 \times 9 =$

$80 + 20 + 10 +$ ___ $=$ **150**

$3 \times 11 =$

$55 + 98 + 73 +$ ___ $=$ **253**

$2 \times 12 =$

$91 + 90 + 99 +$ ___ $=$ **377**

$5 \times 8 =$

# Day 10

Alhumdulillah for: .......................................................................................................

Today's du'a: ...........................................................................
...........................................................................
...........................................................................

## The Fastometer
Color in the amount that you fasted today

## Sadaqah Stars
Write down three good deeds that you did today

☆ ...........................................................................

☆ ...........................................................................

☆ ...........................................................................

## Number of Qur'an pages that you read: ⬡

## Color in the salah that you prayed
*(it doesn't matter if you prayed at home, school or at the masjid)*

Fajr    Dhuhr    'Asr    Maghrib    'Isha

| | | |
|---|---|---|
| Full | 1 | 100% |
| Three-Quarters | | 0.75 |
| 3/4 | | 75% |
| Half | | 0.5 |
| 1/2 | | 50% |
| Quarter | | 0.25 |
| 1/4 | | 25% |

# Coloring Page

# Day 11

Alhumdulillah for: .................................................................

Today's du'a: .................................................................
.................................................................
.................................................................

## The Fastometer
Color in the amount that you fasted today

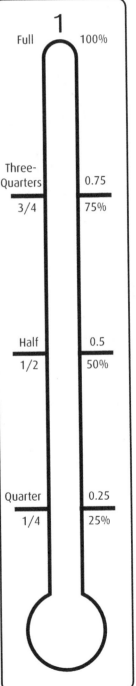

1

Full        100%

Three-Quarters        0.75
3/4        75%

Half        0.5
1/2        50%

Quarter        0.25
1/4        25%

## Sadaqah Stars
Write down three good deeds that you did today

.................................................................

.................................................................

.................................................................

## Number of Qur'an pages that you read: ⬡

## Color in the salah that you prayed
*(it doesn't matter if you prayed at home, school or at the masjid)*

Fajr    Dhuhr    'Asr    Maghrib    'Isha

# Doodles

Ramadan is celebrated by Muslims all around the world. Complete the drawing of our amazing Earth and color it in. Add as much detail as you like, maybe using the ideas at the bottom of the page for inspiration. Some famous landmarks have already been added - can you name them?

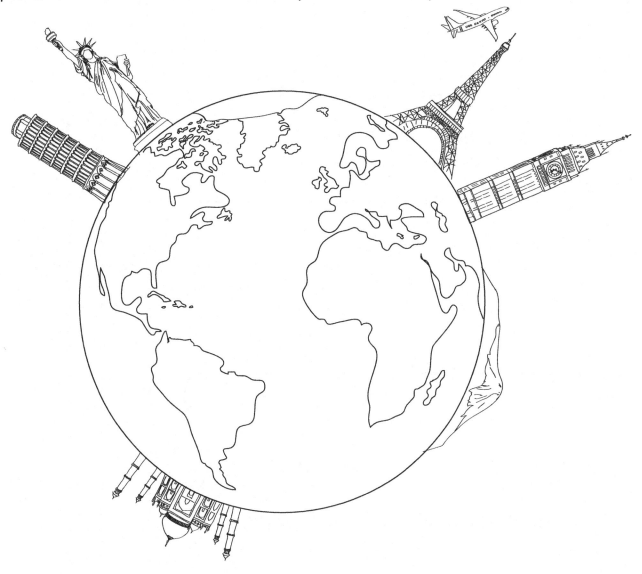

Ideas:

# Day 12

Alhumdulillah for: ..................................................................................................

Today's du'a: ........................................................................
..........................................................................................
..........................................................................................

## The Fastometer
Color in the amount
that you fasted today

## Sadaqah Stars
Write down three good deeds that you did today

☆ ................................................................................

☆ ................................................................................

☆ ................................................................................

# Number of Qur'an pages that you read: ⬡

## Color in the salah that you prayed
*(it doesn't matter if you prayed at home, school or at the masjid)*

Fajr    Dhuhr    'Asr    Maghrib    'Isha

**1**

| Full | 100% |
| Three-Quarters | 0.75 |
| 3/4 | 75% |
| Half | 0.5 |
| 1/2 | 50% |
| Quarter | 0.25 |
| 1/4 | 25% |

# Alphabet Challenge: Sadaqah

Think of a good deed, beginning with each letter of the alphabet. Good deeds are also known as *sadaqah* - which is any act of friendship, love and generosity. Allah rewards you more for your good deeds in Ramadan. We can give sadaqah in many different ways, from giving money in charity to smiling at a stranger.

A _____

B _____

C _____

D _____

E _____

F _____

G _____

H _____

I _____

J _____

K _____

L _____

M _____

N _____

O _____

P _____

Q _____

R _____

S _____

T _____

U _____

V _____

W _____

X _____
If this is too difficult, try a word with X in it

Y _____

Z _____

# Day 13

Alhumdulillah for: ........................................................................................

Today's du'a: ................................................................................
...............................................................................................
...............................................................................................

## The Fastometer
Color in the amount that you fasted today

## Sadaqah Stars
Write down three good deeds that you did today

☆ ............................................................................................

☆ ............................................................................................

☆ ............................................................................................

Number of Qur'an pages that you read: ⬡

## Color in the salah that you prayed
*(it doesn't matter if you prayed at home, school or at the masjid)*

Fajr    Dhuhr    'Asr    Maghrib    'Isha

**The Fastometer**

| | 1 | |
|---|---|---|
| Full | | 100% |
| Three-Quarters | | 0.75 |
| | 3/4 | 75% |
| Half | | 0.5 |
| | 1/2 | 50% |
| Quarter | | 0.25 |
| | 1/4 | 25% |

# Unscrambler

Unscramble the letters to work out the Ramadan-themed words.

STADE        _ _ _ _ _

FITSANG        _ _ _ _ _ _ _

QASHAAD        _ _ _ _ _ _ _

RATAIF        _ _ _ _ _ _

SQUOME        _ _ _ _ _ _

NAQUR        _ _ _ _ _

DRAMAAN        _ _ _ _ _ _ _

SHAAL        _ _ _ _ _

AUD        _ _ _

JUTHJAUD        _ _ _ _ _ _ _ _

WATHAIR        _ _ _ _ _ _ _

RICHATY        _ _ _ _ _ _ _

SKINENDS        _ _ _ _ _ _ _ _

# Day 14

Alhumdulillah for: ...........................................................................................

Today's du'a: .........................................................................
........................................................................................................
........................................................................................................

## The Fastometer
Color in the amount
that you fasted today

**1**

Full        100%

Three-Quarters    0.75
3/4        75%

Half        0.5
1/2        50%

Quarter      0.25
1/4        25%

## Sadaqah Stars
Write down three good deeds that you did today

☆ ........................................................................

☆ ........................................................................

☆ ........................................................................

## Number of Qur'an pages that you read: ⬡

## Color in the salah that you prayed
*(it doesn't matter if you prayed at home, school or at the masjid)*

Fajr     Dhuhr     'Asr     Maghrib     'Isha

# Design Time

Design a poster encouraging people to pray more Qur'an:

# Day 15

Alhumdulillah for: .............................................................

Today's du'a: .............................................................
.............................................................
.............................................................

## The Fastometer
Color in the amount that you fasted today

| | 1 | |
|---|---|---|
| Full | | 100% |
| Three-Quarters | | 0.75 |
| | 3/4 | 75% |
| Half | | 0.5 |
| | 1/2 | 50% |
| Quarter | | 0.25 |
| | 1/4 | 25% |

## Sadaqah Stars
Write down three good deeds that you did today

.............................................................

.............................................................

.............................................................

## Number of Qur'an pages that you read:

## Color in the salah that you prayed
*(it doesn't matter if you prayed at home, school or at the masjid)*

Fajr   Dhuhr   'Asr   Maghrib   'Isha

# Good Deeds Task

Most of us love watching birds, especially in our own gardens. One way to see more birds is to make your garden more attractive to them. If you want to attract birds to your garden, then feeding them will help.

With just a few simple ingredients that are easily available, you can make these Ramadan-themed "tweets" for your feathered friends.

## You will need:

4 cups wild bird food or bird seed

¾ cup plain flour

3 tablespoons light corn syrup

½ cup water

Star shaped cookie cutters

Wool or twine

Drinking straw

## Method:

1. In a large bowl mix together the flour, corn syrup and water

2. Add the bird seed and mix until well blended

3. Line your work surface with wax paper. Press the bird seed mixture into the cookie cutters. Use a straw to make a hole but be sure not to make the hole too close to the top or the ornament will break.

4. Leave to dry for 4-6 hours or overnight, turning them often so that they can dry on both sides.

5. String the ornaments with the wool, then hang in a tree or bush.

# Day 16

Alhumdulillah for: .................................................................................................

Today's du'a: ...................................................................................
...................................................................................
...................................................................................

## The Fastometer
Color in the amount
that you fasted today

## Sadaqah Stars
Write down three good deeds that you did today

☆ ...................................................................................

☆ ...................................................................................

☆ ...................................................................................

Number of Qur'an pages that you read: ⬡

## Color in the salah that you prayed
*(it doesn't matter if you prayed at home, school or at the masjid)*

Fajr    Dhuhr    'Asr    Maghrib    'Isha

**The Fastometer**

1

Full — 100%

Three-Quarters — 0.75
3/4 — 75%

Half — 0.5
1/2 — 50%

Quarter — 0.25
1/4 — 25%

# Story Time

Write down your favorite story about one of the prophets عليه السلام.

_____

_____

_____

_____

_____

_____

_____

_____

_____

_____

_____

_____

_____

_____

_____

_____

_____

_____

_____

_____

# Day 17

Alhumdulillah for: ...........................................................................

Today's du'a: ...................................................................
...........................................................................................
...........................................................................................

## The Fastometer
Color in the amount that you fasted today

## Sadaqah Stars
Write down three good deeds that you did today

☆ ...................................................................

☆ ...................................................................

☆ ...................................................................

Number of Qur'an pages that you read: ⬡

## Color in the salah that you prayed
*(it doesn't matter if you prayed at home, school or at the masjid)*

Fajr   Dhuhr   'Asr   Maghrib   'Isha

| | | |
|---|---|---|
| Full | 1 | 100% |
| Three-Quarters | | 0.75 |
| 3/4 | | 75% |
| Half | | 0.5 |
| 1/2 | | 50% |
| Quarter | | 0.25 |
| 1/4 | | 25% |

# Design Time

Design a poster about your favorite story of one of the Prophets العَلَيْهِمُ السَّلَام.

# Day 18

Alhumdulillah for: .................................................................................................

Today's du'a: .................................................................................................
.................................................................................................
.................................................................................................

## The Fastometer
Color in the amount that you fasted today

## Sadaqah Stars
Write down three good deeds that you did today

.................................................................................................

.................................................................................................

.................................................................................................

Number of Qur'an pages that you read:

## Color in the salah that you prayed
*(it doesn't matter if you prayed at home, school or at the masjid)*

Fajr    Dhuhr    'Asr    Maghrib    'Isha

| Full | 1 | 100% |
| Three-Quarters | | 0.75 |
| 3/4 | | 75% |
| Half | | 0.5 |
| 1/2 | | 50% |
| Quarter | | 0.25 |
| 1/4 | | 25% |

# Interview

Answer the questions about the people you are grateful for.

One adult I am grateful for is: _____

Because: _____

_____

One friend I am grateful for is: _____

Because: _____

_____

One teacher I am grateful for is: _____

Because: _____

_____

One of my heroes is: _____

Because: _____

_____

One person really special to me is: _____

Because: _____

_____

# Day 19

Alhumdulillah for: .......................................................................................

Today's du'a: ..............................................................................

.......................................................................................

.......................................................................................

## The Fastometer
Color in the amount
that you fasted today

## Sadaqah Stars
Write down three good deeds that you did today

☆ ..............................................................................

☆ ..............................................................................

☆ ..............................................................................

Number of Qur'an pages that you read: ⬡

## Color in the salah that you prayed
*(it doesn't matter if you prayed at home, school or at the masjid)*

Fajr

Dhuhr

'Asr

Maghrib

'Isha

1

Full          100%

Three-        0.75
Quarters
3/4           75%

Half          0.5
1/2           50%

Quarter       0.25
1/4           25%

# Alphabet Challenge: Food

Write down all the foods you enjoy, beginning with each letter of the alphabet.

A _____

B _____

C _____

D _____

E _____

F _____

G _____

H _____

I _____

J _____

K _____

L _____

M _____

N _____

O _____

P _____

Q _____

R _____

S _____

T _____

U _____

V _____

W _____

X _____
If this is too difficult, try a word with X in it

Y _____

Z _____

# Day 20 Alhumdulillah for: .....................................................

Today's du'a: ...................................................
.............................................................................
.............................................................................

## The Fastometer
Color in the amount that you fasted today

## Sadaqah Stars
Write down three good deeds that you did today

..................................................

..................................................

..................................................

Number of Qur'an pages that you read: ⬡

## Color in the salah that you prayed
*(it doesn't matter if you prayed at home, school or at the masjid)*

Fajr    Dhuhr    'Asr    Maghrib    'Isha

**1**

| | | |
|---|---|---|
| Full | | 100% |
| Three-Quarters | 0.75 | |
| 3/4 | | 75% |
| Half | 0.5 | |
| 1/2 | | 50% |
| Quarter | 0.25 | |
| 1/4 | | 25% |

# Coloring Page

# Day 21

Alhumdulillah for: ...........................................................................................

Today's du'a: ...........................................................................

...........................................................................................

...........................................................................................

## The Fastometer
Color in the amount
that you fasted today

## Sadaqah Stars
Write down three good deeds that you did today

☆ ...........................................................................

☆ ...........................................................................

☆ ...........................................................................

Number of Qur'an pages that you read: ⬡

## Color in the salah that you prayed
*(it doesn't matter if you prayed at home, school or at the masjid)*

Fajr    Dhuhr    'Asr    Maghrib    'Isha

**1**

Full — 100%

Three-Quarters — 0.75 / 3/4 — 75%

Half — 0.5 / 1/2 — 50%

Quarter — 0.25 / 1/4 — 25%

# Missing Words

Fill in the blanks with the correct words, all about Laylat ul Qadr

Laylat ul Qadr is the Night of P____.

It is one of the nights of the last t__ days of Ramadan, and on this night the blessings and m____ of Allah ﷻ are generous, s___ are forgiven and d___ are accepted.

"Verily! We have sent it (this Q____) down in the night of Al-Qadr.
And what will make you know what the night of Al-Qadr is?
The night of Al-Qadr is better than a t_____ months
Therein descend the a_____ and the Ruh by Allah's Permission with all Decrees,
Peace! Until the appearance of dawn." (Qur'an: 97:1-5)

'Aisha ﷺ related that the P_____ ﷺ said: Look for Laylat ul Qadr on an o__ numbered night during the last ten nights of Ramadan. (Bukhari)

'Aisha ﷺ reported: I asked: "O M_____ of Allah! If I realise Laylat ul Qadr, what should I supplicate in it?" He replied, "You should supplicate:

ALLAHUMMA INNAKA 'AFUWWUN, TUHIBBUL-'AFWA, FA'FU 'ANNI

(O Allah, You are Most Forgiving, and You love forgiveness; so f_____ me)."
(At-Tirmidhi)

# Day 22

Alhumdulillah for: ....................................................................................

Today's du'a: ....................................................................................

....................................................................................

....................................................................................

## The Fastometer
Color in the amount that you fasted today

## Sadaqah Stars
Write down three good deeds that you did today

☆ ....................................................................................

☆ ....................................................................................

☆ ....................................................................................

Number of Qur'an pages that you read: ⬡

## Color in the salah that you prayed
*(it doesn't matter if you prayed at home, school or at the masjid)*

Fajr    Dhuhr    'Asr    Maghrib    'Isha

**1**
Full    100%

Three-Quarters    0.75
3/4    75%

Half    0.5
1/2    50%

Quarter    0.25
1/4    25%

# Design Time

Design a poster telling people all about Laylat ul Qadr:

# Day 23 Alhumdulillah for: ...........................................................................

Today's du'a: ...........................................................
...........................................................................................
...........................................................................................

## The Fastometer
Color in the amount
that you fasted today

## Sadaqah Stars
Write down three good deeds that you did today

Number of Qur'an pages that you read:

## Color in the salah that you prayed
*(it doesn't matter if you prayed at home, school or at the masjid)*

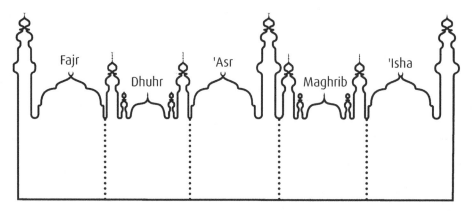

Fajr    Dhuhr    'Asr    Maghrib    'Isha

| | 1 | |
| Full | | 100% |
| Three-Quarters | | 0.75 |
| 3/4 | | 75% |
| Half | | 0.5 |
| 1/2 | | 50% |
| Quarter | | 0.25 |
| 1/4 | | 25% |

# Good Deeds Task

Make strawberry ice cream - a lovely cold treat to share with your family at Iftaar.

This fresh strawberry ice cream with bits of berries in is absolutely delicious! It's also a very mild pink color, not like store-bought strawberry ice cream, because it doesn't have all those artificial colors and flavorings in.

## Ingredients:

500g strawberries, hulled

200g milk powder

200ml fresh cream

1 cup milk

½ cup sugar

## Method:

. Add 250 grams of strawberries into a blender and puree.

. Add the rest of the ingredients and blend for two minutes.

. Pour the mixture into a container, then put it in the freezer. After 1 hour take it out and whisk with a fork. Put it back in the freezer, then take out after an hour and whisk with a fork again. Repeat this another two times so that you have whisked it four times in total.

. In the meantime, pulse or mince the other half of the strawberries (250 grams) in a food processor, or chop with a knife. You will love the bits of berries in the ice cream, so it is worth the effort.

. Add them into the semi-set ice cream, folding them in carefully. Put it back into the freezer, and leave to freeze.

. Scoop it out when you're ready to eat, and enjoy!

# Day 24 Alhumdulillah for: ......................................................................

Today's du'a: ............................................................
................................................................................
................................................................................

## The Fastometer
Color in the amount that you fasted today

## Sadaqah Stars
Write down three good deeds that you did today

☆ ...................................................................

☆ ...................................................................

☆ ...................................................................

# Number of Qur'an pages that you read: ⬡

# Color in the salah that you prayed
*(it doesn't matter if you prayed at home, school or at the masjid)*

Fajr

Dhuhr

'Asr

Maghrib

'Isha

| | 1 | |
|---|---|---|
| Full | | 100% |
| Three-Quarters | 0.75 | |
| 3/4 | | 75% |
| Half | 0.5 | |
| 1/2 | | 50% |
| Quarter | 0.25 | |
| 1/4 | | 25% |

# Doodles

Color in these sweet treats, then draw your favorite 'Eid dessert in the centre.

# Day 25

Alhumdulillah for: _____

Today's du'a: _____
_____
_____

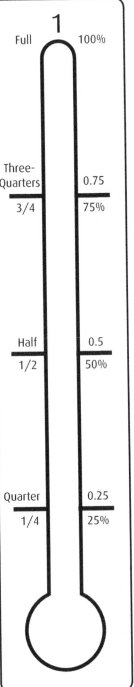

## The Fastometer
Color in the amount that you fasted today

1
Full · 100%

Three-Quarters · 0.75
3/4 · 75%

Half · 0.5
1/2 · 50%

Quarter · 0.25
1/4 · 25%

## Sadaqah Stars
Write down three good deeds that you did today

_____

_____

_____

Number of Qur'an pages that you read: ⬡

## Color in the salah that you prayed
*(it doesn't matter if you prayed at home, school or at the masjid)*

Fajr    Dhuhr    'Asr    Maghrib    'Isha

# Wordsearch

All about Eid.

| | | | | | | | | | | | | | | | |
|---|---|---|---|---|---|---|---|---|---|---|---|---|---|---|---|
| A | G | D | H | H | J | I | W | T | Y | U | O | P | S | A | L | A |
| F | C | H | J | K | A | F | B | C | Q | E | T | E | U | I | O | P |
| F | H | E | M | O | N | O | O | K | L | A | Q | U | E | H | J | O |
| H | S | L | L | F | E | B | I | O | C | A | K | A | H | I | K | L |
| L | H | R | E | E | M | A | A | R | D | I | D | A | M | U | D | O |
| E | A | H | Y | S | B | L | A | A | C | L | A | O | A | B | I | K |
| G | R | A | N | T | M | R | V | Y | H | Z | H | X | S | O | O | H |
| O | I | I | A | I | O | X | A | V | A | T | A | N | J | K | Q | U |
| P | N | O | O | V | S | G | H | T | R | G | P | U | I | G | I | T |
| G | G | E | B | A | Q | M | X | C | I | H | P | J | D | V | K | B |
| I | L | E | R | L | U | H | O | V | T | O | I | B | N | B | L | A |
| F | A | M | I | L | Y | Q | W | O | Y | E | N | R | T | N | P | H |
| T | Z | B | N | J | C | L | O | T | N | H | E | W | S | F | M | O |
| S | F | H | I | L | Y | E | I | Y | D | S | S | A | L | A | H | O |
| A | P | C | L | O | T | H | E | S | V | A | S | F | G | H | N | L |
| C | H | J | A | R | T | C | H | A | P | A | R | T | Y | R | I | T |
| I | O | H | A | N | N | O | E | R | T | Y | U | H | J | S | A | Y |

| | | |
|---|---|---|
| Celebration | Festival | Masjid |
| Charity | Food | Moon |
| Clothes | Gifts | Party |
| Eid | Happiness | Salah |
| Family | Khutbah | Sharing |

# Day 26 Alhumdulillah for: .............................................................................

Today's du'a: ..................................................................................
..................................................................................................................
..................................................................................................................

## The Fastometer
Color in the amount
that you fasted today

## Sadaqah Stars
Write down three good deeds that you did today

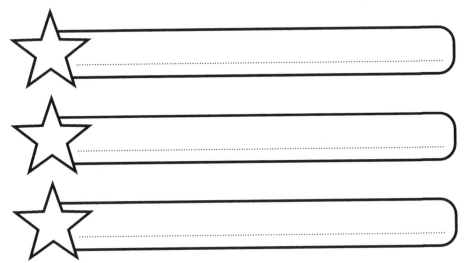

Number of Qur'an pages that you read: ⬡

## Color in the salah that you prayed
*(it doesn't matter if you prayed at home, school or at the masjid)*

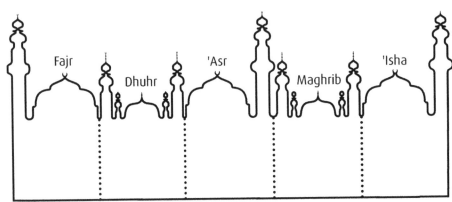

Fajr   Dhuhr   'Asr   Maghrib   'Isha

1
Full          100%

Three-
Quarters      0.75
3/4           75%

Half          0.5
1/2           50%

Quarter       0.25
1/4           25%

# Alphabet Challenge: 'Eid

Write down words all about 'Eid, beginning with each letter of the alphabet.

A _____

B _____

C _____

D _____

E _____

F _____

G _____

H _____

I _____

J _____

K _____

L _____

M _____

N _____

O _____

P _____

Q _____

R _____

S _____

T _____

U _____

V _____

W _____

X _____
If this is too difficult, try a word with X in it

Y _____

Z _____

# Day 27

Alhumdulillah for: .................................................................

Today's du'a: ...............................................................
....................................................................................
....................................................................................

## The Fastometer
Color in the amount that you fasted today

## Sadaqah Stars
Write down three good deeds that you did today

Number of Qur'an pages that you read: ⬡

## Color in the salah that you prayed
*(it doesn't matter if you prayed at home, school or at the masjid)*

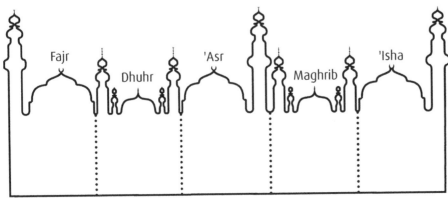

Fajr  Dhuhr  'Asr  Maghrib  'Isha

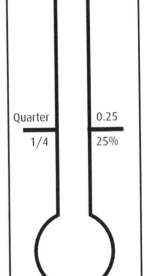

1
Full          100%

Three-Quarters    0.75
3/4            75%

Half           0.5
1/2            50%

Quarter        0.25
1/4            25%

# Design Time

Draw a poster advertising a community 'Eid party:

# Day 28 Alhumdulillah for: .......................................................

Today's du'a: .......................................................
.......................................................
.......................................................

## Sadaqah Stars
### Write down three good deeds that you did today

☆ .......................................................

☆ .......................................................

☆ .......................................................

# Number of Qur'an pages that you read: ⬡

# Color in the salah that you prayed
*(it doesn't matter if you prayed at home, school or at the masjid)*

Fajr    Dhuhr    'Asr    Maghrib    'Isha

## The Fastometer
Color in the amount
that you fasted today

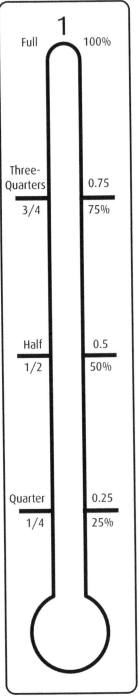

1
Full          100%

Three-
Quarters      0.75
3/4           75%

Half          0.5
1/2           50%

Quarter       0.25
1/4           25%

# Doodles

Color in these gift, then draw your ideal 'Eid present in the centre.

# Day 29 Alhumdulillah for: .................................................

Today's du'a: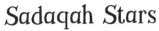
..................................................................................
..................................................................................

## The Fastometer
Color in the amount
that you fasted today

## Sadaqah Stars
Write down three good deeds that you did today

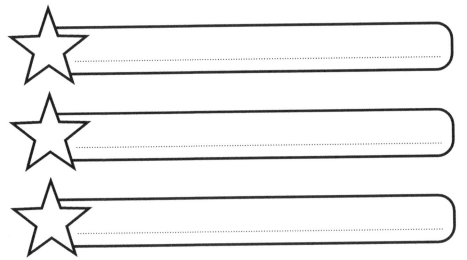

Number of Qur'an pages that you read:

## Color in the salah that you prayed
*(it doesn't matter if you prayed at home, school or at the masjid)*

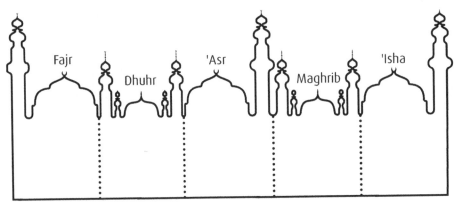

Fajr    Dhuhr    'Asr    Maghrib    'Isha

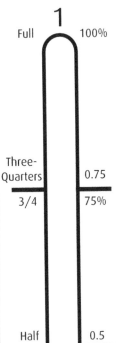

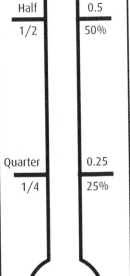

| | |
|---|---|
| **1** | |
| Full | 100% |
| Three-Quarters | 0.75 |
| 3/4 | 75% |
| Half | 0.5 |
| 1/2 | 50% |
| Quarter | 0.25 |
| 1/4 | 25% |

# Good Deeds Task

Eid is almost here and most likely your family have been busy preparing lots of food as part of the celebrations! How about contributing with a delicious fruity drink to wash it all down with?

## Ingredients:

1 cup concentrated lemonade

6 oz concentrated orange juice

2 cups cranberry juice

3 cups water

¼ cup super-fine sugar

2 litres lemon-lime soda, chilled

Freshly sliced fruit such as lemons, oranges, strawberries and pineapples

## Method:

1. Add the lemonade, orange juice, cranberry juice, sugar and water to a container that has a lid. Stir until all the sugar has dissolved.

2. Cover and chill the mixture for 1-2 hours.

3. When you are ready to serve, add the soda, ice and fruit, then pour into a jug to serve.

# Day 30 Alhumdulillah for: ..................................................................

Today's du'a: ......................................................
................................................................................
................................................................................

## Sadaqah Stars
Write down three good deeds that you did today

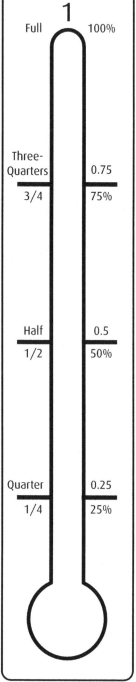

**The Fastometer**
Color in the amount that you fasted today

| | 1 | |
| Full | | 100% |
| Three-Quarters | | 0.75 |
| 3/4 | | 75% |
| Half | | 0.5 |
| 1/2 | | 50% |
| Quarter | | 0.25 |
| 1/4 | | 25% |

Number of Qur'an pages that you read: ⬡

## Color in the salah that you prayed
*(it doesn't matter if you prayed at home, school or at the masjid)*

Fajr    Dhuhr    'Asr    Maghrib    'Isha

# Missing Words

Fill in the blanks and learn all about 'Eid.

We know it's the end of Ramadan when the new m___ is sighted. The day after Ramadan ends is called E__ ul Fitr. On this day, fasting is f_____.

Eid ul Fitr is the first day of the month of S_____.

Muslims are not only c_____ the end of fasting, but also thanking A____ for His help.

During Eid-ul-Fitr Muslims dress in their finest c_____, give g____ to each other and spend time with their friends and f_____.

At Eid it is compulsory to give a set amount of money to c_____ to be used to help poor people buy n__ clothes and f___ so that they can also celebrate.

# Bonus Good Deed Task: Charity Gift

Fill an empty box or gift bag with as many of the following items as you can, then give to a homeless person in your local area:

- Bottle of water · Blanket · Painkillers · Snacks (e.g. crackers, crisps or chocolate)
- Apples · Books · Toiletries · Woolly scarf, hat and gloves · Socks · Tissues
- Wipes · Plasters · Toothbrush & toothpaste · Gift voucher for a local coffee shop

# Answers:

## Day 2: True or False

1. False. It comes forward by approximately 10 days each year. 2. False. You have to fast from sunrise to sunset. 3. False. The morning meal is called Suhoor. 4. True 5. False. Your rewards are multiplied by more than 700. 6. True. 7. True 8. True. 9. False. Ramadan is the ninth month. 10. True.

## Day 3: Math Task

1: 4 days  2: 2 days  3: One week  4: 30 weeks  5: Twice

## Day 7: All About Ramadan Wordsearch

| | | | | | | | | | | | | | | |
|---|---|---|---|---|---|---|---|---|---|---|---|---|---|---|
| S | Z | G | H | K | L | F | T | U | H | A | J | J | U | D | G | H |
| Q | A | Y | U | I | O | A | A | V | M | Z | X | D | T | H | J | J |
| A | K | D | A | T | E | S | S | U | H | A | O | P | Q | S | M | L |
| C | A | F | H | D | T | T | G | S | Z | Q | S | E | U | K | J | K |
| N | T | P | R | G | U | I | S | U | X | C | V | J | R | I | M | B |
| Q | T | U | N | W | H | N | V | H | W | X | Q | Y | I | N | Z | A |
| U | B | C | F | A | A | G | D | O | E | G | I | H | N | D | J | M |
| R | E | V | E | L | A | T | I | O | N | P | R | H | O | N | L | N |
| A | I | O | R | P | J | Z | Q | R | X | G | T | O | O | E | X | S |
| N | F | U | R | A | Y | X | U | Z | A | F | A | B | J | S | M | A |
| N | T | Q | D | I | T | O | P | O | F | H | R | Z | Q | S | S | L |
| O | A | E | F | D | S | G | I | F | T | S | A | B | A | I | A | A |
| R | A | M | A | D | A | N | H | G | F | E | W | C | D | O | L | R |
| P | R | S | U | P | P | L | I | C | A | T | I | O | N | N | A | O |
| R | S | U | D | O | O | W | F | C | V | B | H | N | M | A | H | O |
| S | F | C | H | A | R | I | T | Y | Y | N | M | U | I | O | H | R |
| Q | O | R | A | B | D | N | J | K | T | Y | S | G | H | W | N | B |

## Day 8: Missing Words

ninth | calendar | world | sunrise | sunset | pillars | Qur'an | Muhammad | Power | bad | better praying | whole | special | Suhoor | Iftaar | poor | eat | waste | kind

# Day 9: Math Task

ADDITIONS: 1. **10**  2. **25**  3. **40**  4. **27**  5. **97**   MULTIPLICATIONS: 6. **28**  7. **81**  8. **33**  9. **24**  10. **40**

# Day 13: Unscrambler

DATES | FASTING | SADAQAH | IFTAAR | MOSQUE | QURAN | RAMADAN | SALAH | DUA |
TUHAJJUD | TARAWIH | CHARITY | KINDNESS

# Day 21: Missing Words

Power | mercy | sins | du'as | Qur'an | thousand | angels | Prophet | odd | Messenger | forgive

# Day 25: All About Eid Wordsearch

```
A G D H H J I W T Y U O P S A L A
F C H J K A F B C Q E T E U I O P
F H E M O N O O K L A Q U E H J O
H S H L F E B I O C A K A H I K L
L H R E E M A A R D I D A M U D O
E A H Y S B L A A C L A O A B I K
G R A N T M R V Y H Z H X S O O H
O I I A I O X A V A T A N J K Q U
P N O O V S G H T R G P U I G I T
G G E B A Q M X C I H P J D V K B
I L E R L U H O V T O I B N B L A
F A M I L Y Q W O Y E N R T N P H
T Z B N J C L O T N H E W S F M O
S F H I L Y E I Y D S S A L A H O
A P C L O T H E S V A S F G H N L
C H J A R T C H A P A R T Y R I T
I O H A N N O E R T Y U H J S A Y
```

# Day 30: Missing Words

moon | Eid | forbidden | Shawwal | celebrating | Allah | clothes | gifts | family | charity
new | food

If you enjoyed this book, check out the next edition of Pray & Play
and more activity books, at:

# reyoflightdesign.com/store
www.etsy.com/uk/shop/reyoflightdesign

Other products include:

Children's Journals · Annual Planners (including Hijri dated) · Academic Planners
Small Business Planners · Salah Trackers (adults, teens and kids) · Qur'an Journals
Ramadan Planners (adults and teens) · Travel Journals (adults/teens and kids)
Health Diaries · Notebooks

Made in the USA
Coppell, TX
18 March 2021

51905318R00039